LOOM
Magic!

25 Awesome, Never-Before-Seen Designs for
an Amazing Rainbow of Projects

John McCann
&
Becky Thomas

Sky Pony Press
New York

Sky Pony Press books may be purchased in bulk at special discounts for sales promotion, corporate gifts, fund-raising, or educational purposes. Special editions can also be created to specifications. For details, contact the Special Sales Department, Sky Pony Press, 307 West 36th Street, 11th Floor, New York, NY 10018 or info@skyhorsepublishing.com.

Sky Pony® is a registered trademark of Skyhorse Publishing, Inc.®, a Delaware corporation.

Visit our website at www.skyponypress.com.

10 9 8 7 6 5 4 3 2 1

Manufactured in the United States of America, October 2013
This product conforms to CPSIA 2008

Library of Congress Cataloguing-in-Publication Data is available on file.

ISBN: 978-1-62914-334-7

CONTENTS

ACKNOWLEDGMENTS

We would like to give many thank-yous to Kelsie Besaw, our champion editor, and to everyone at Skyhorse who worked with remarkable speed on this project. Thank you to Bill Wolfsthal, Tony Lyons, and Linda Biagi for putting this project together. Special thanks to Allan Penn, for your great photography and creative coaching, as well as to Holly Schmidt, for keeping us on track and making delicious sandwiches, and Monica Sweeney, for making sure everything made sense.

Our enormous gratitude goes to Jax Kordes as well as Olivia Sahagian for contributing such wonderful and unique projects to this book. Your ideas made this book extra special!

To all of the wonderful faces of *Loom Magic!*: Thank you Lucy Bartlett, Sally Brunelle, Quisi Cohen, Charlotte Penn, Noah Rotner, and Caleb and Owen Schmidt. This book would not be the same without you!

OCTO BRACELET

This pattern uses eight bands to make a repeating circle shape: that's why it's called "octo"! Or maybe it's because you'll want to make at least eight bracelets with this fun new stitch!

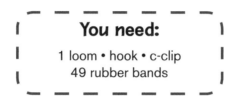

You need:

1 loom • hook • c-clip
49 rubber bands

1. Set up the loom with three rows of pegs, with the middle row set forward one peg (toward you). Loop a rubber band over the middle peg closest to you, then connect it to the peg one up and to the left. Loop another band around this peg and connect it to the peg above it. Loop one band around the peg you ended on, and connect it to the third middle peg. Start at the middle peg closest to you. Loop a band around this peg and connect it to the next peg up and to the right. Finish the rest of the circle as you did with the pegs on the left.

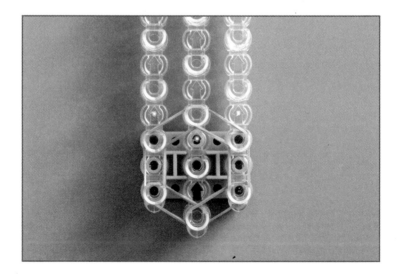

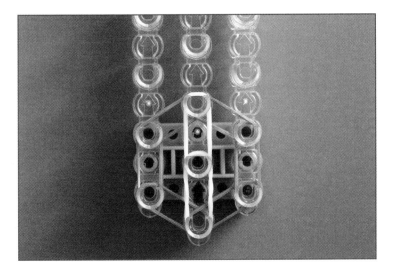

2. Loop a band around the middle peg closest to you, and connect it to the middle peg above it. Repeat with the next peg up.

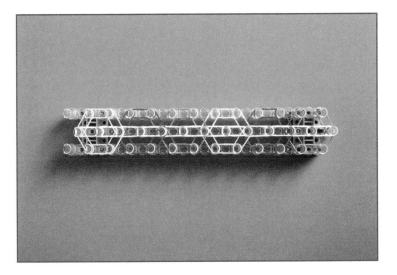

3. Starting on the middle peg three pegs up the loom, repeat steps 2–4, looping the left half of the circle, then the right, then looping the pegs up the middle. Continue up the loom, making 6 total circles. Loop one band around the middle peg furthest from you, then connect it to the peg up and to the right.

4. Turn the loom around so that the arrow is pointing towards you. Starting with the peg closest to you on the right, hook the second loop down on the peg, and pull it up and off the peg, looping it back onto the peg where the other end is still looped. Continue looping the rest the pegs in  the same way, working your way up the loom. When you have looped all the rubber bands back onto their starting pegs, turn the loom again so that the arrow is facing away from you, and find the first peg you looped. Use your hook to grab all of the bands on this peg, and loop another band through these bands and pull it tight. You can also use a c-clip for this.

5. Remove the bracelet from the loom. Connect the two ends with a c-clip.

STRAIGHTAWAY BRACELET

This unique design will wow your friends, and it's a breeze to make! It will fit right in with the stack of bracelets on your arm!

You need:

1 loom • hook
36 rubber bands

1. Set up the loom with the red arrow pointing away from you and the middle row set one peg closer to you. Loop a band over the middle peg closest to you, then connect it to the next peg up and to the left. Loop another band over this second peg, and connect it to the peg above. Continue to double loop in this way all the way up the left side of the loom. Do the same on the right side of the loom.

2. Loop one band over the last peg in the row on the left, and connect it to the last peg in the middle row. Do the same with the last peg on the right.

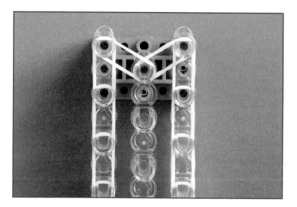

3. Loop a band over the first middle peg, and connect it to the middle peg above it. Loop a band over the closest peg on the left, and connect it to the second middle peg (where you ended your last loop). Loop another band over the closest peg on the right, and connect it to the second middle peg.

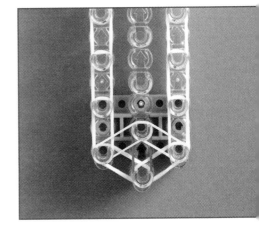

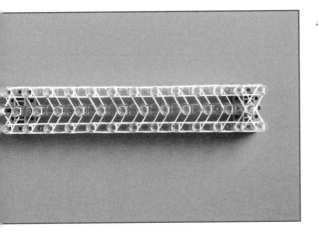

4. Move up to the second middle peg on the loom, and repeat step 3. Continue up the loom in this way until you reach the end.

5. Double-loop a rubber band and put it on the top middle peg.

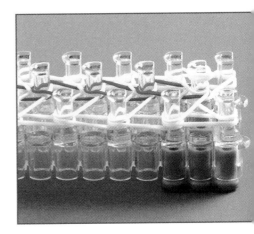

6. Turn the loom around so that the arrow is pointing toward you. Starting with the second middle peg, hook the second band on the peg and pull it up and off, looping back onto the peg where it started. Continue looping up the middle of the loom.

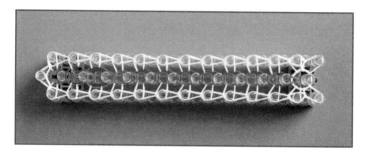

7. Start at the middle peg closest to you. Loop the edges in the same way. Loop the bands off this peg and back onto the first pegs on the left and right. Loop in the same way all the way up the left and right of the loom.

8. Remove your bracelet from the loom.

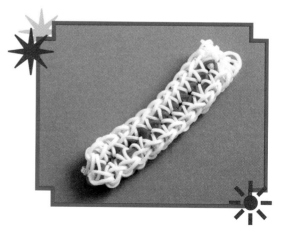

PiNNACLE BRACELET

This pattern is made by repeating a triangle shape all the way up the loom. It comes together quick, and it's sure to be a favorite!

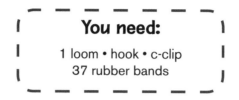

You need:

1 loom • hook • c-clip
37 rubber bands

1. Set up your loom with three rows of pegs set up squarely. Loop a band around the peg closest to you on the right, and connect it to the closest peg on the left (connecting all three pegs in the row). Loop a band around the closest peg on the right, then connect it up to the middle peg in the next row. Do the same with the closest peg on the left.

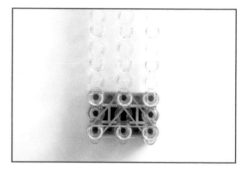

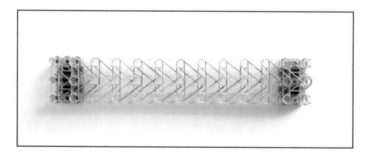

2. Starting on the right peg in the second row, repeat the pattern you made in step 1. Continue until you reach the end of the loom.

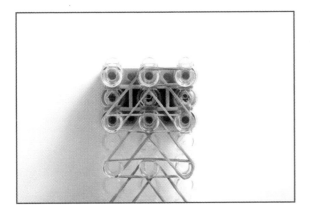

3. Loop a band around the middle peg in the last row, and connect it to the next peg to the right.

4. Turn the loom so the arrow is facing you. Starting with the middle peg, hook the second band from the top and pull it up and off, looping it back to the peg where it started. Move to the next row of pegs, and loop the bands from the corner pegs of

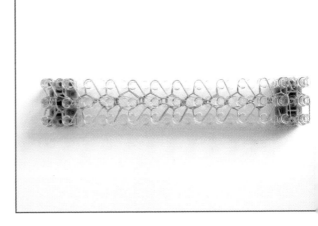

the triangle onto the center peg in the same row. Continue looping this way until you've finished the loom.

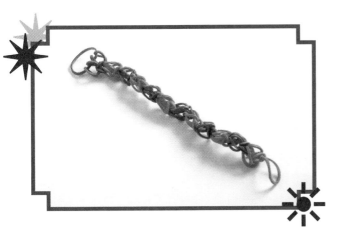

5. Secure the loops from the final peg with a c-clip, and remove your project from the loom.

SQUISHY POOF BALL

This squishy poof ball is so much fun, you won't want to make just one. You can stick these cool little poof balls on your bracelets, your bike handlebars, or the zipper of your backpack, or you can toss them around with your friends! For even more fun, check out the Poof Ball Slingshot on page 27!

You need:

scissors • 1 loom • hook • c-clip
32 rubber bands

1. Set up your loom as shown, with two rows of pegs separated by an empty space between them.

2. Take two rubber bands and tie them together. Repeat until you've used up all but two of the rubber bands.

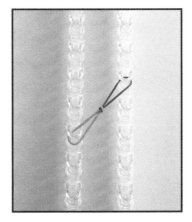

3. Loop one of your tied rubber bands into the loom at an angle.

4. Take another tied rubber band and loop it into the loom at an opposite angle so the knots overlap and the bands make an X shape.

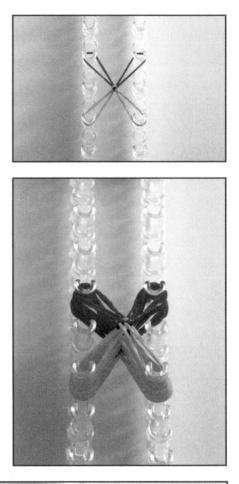

5. Repeat until you've used up all of your tied rubber bands.

6. Loop one of your leftover rubber bands around your X from top to bottom. Pull one end through the other, and pull it tight.

7. Secure the loop with a c-clip.

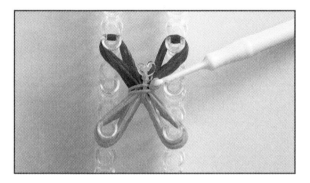

8. Loop your last rubber band around your X in the other direction (right to left), and pull it tight.

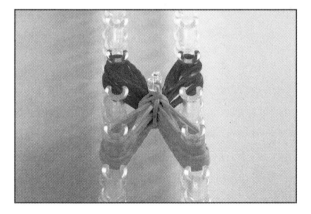

9. Hook the loop into the c-clip.

10. Remove your bands from the loom.

11. Cut through the loops at the end of your X. (Be careful not to cut the loops tied around the middle!)

12. Fluff, squish, and squeeze your poof ball to make it round.

Notes: Stack more knotted rubber bands for an even bigger ball! You can also change up your color combinations to make different patterns.

MUSTACHE

Once you make this cool creation, you can twirl your mustache to look just like an evil villain or a video game superhero! Wear it for Halloween, a school play, or when you just feel like goofing around!

You need:

2 looms • 2 c-clips
about 70 rubber bands

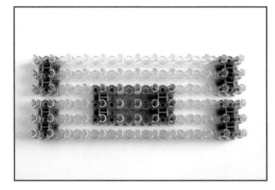

1. Begin with two looms side by side. The pegs should be lined up squarely with the arrows pointing left.

2. Start at the top row all the way to the right. Loop a band around the top right peg, then loop the other end around the peg below it.

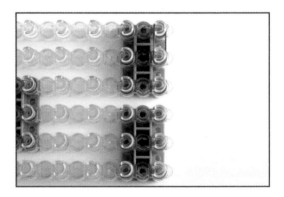

3. Loop a band around the second peg down, and attach it to the peg below, as you did before.

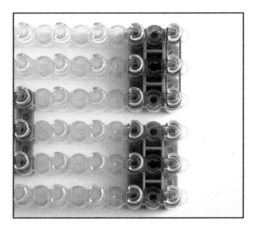

4. Loop another band around the second peg down on the right, and attach this diagonally to the peg one down and to the left. Do the same with the peg just below.

5. Loop a rubber band over the peg where you ended your first diagonal band, then connect it to the peg below, where you ended your second diagonal band.

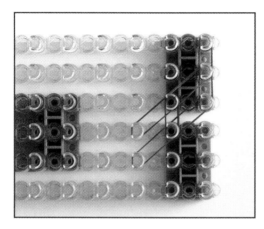

6. Connect a rubber band to the peg where you started your last band, then loop it diagonally to the peg one down and to the left. Do the same starting from the peg below.

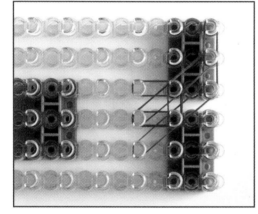

7. Starting at the same peg as the last step, hook a rubber band to connect the peg to the next peg to the left. Do the same with the peg below.

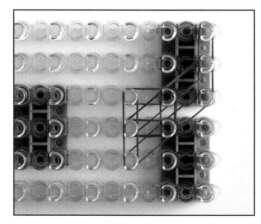

8. Hook a band over the peg where you ended your top horizontal line, then loop the other end over the peg below. Loop a band around the next peg down, and connect it to the peg below.

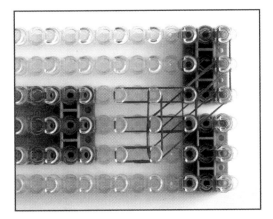

9. On each of the three pegs you connected, loop a rubber band over the peg and connect it to the next peg to the left.

10. Starting again at the top of your connected three pegs, hook a rubber band to the peg and connect it diagonally to the peg below and to the left. Repeat for the next two pegs down.

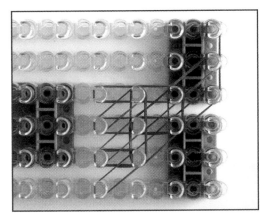

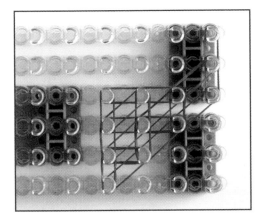

11. Hook a band around the peg on the bottom row where you ended your bottom diagonal loop, and connect it to the peg above it. Repeat with the next two pegs up, connecting four pegs total.

12. On each of the four pegs you just connected, loop a rubber band and connect the peg to the next peg to the left.

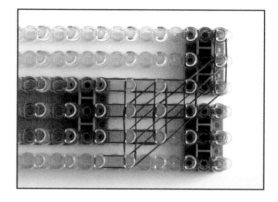

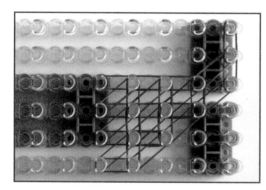

13. Starting at the top of your four connected pegs, loop a rubber band and connect it diagonally to the peg one down and to the left. Do the same for the next two pegs down.

14. From the bottom peg (five from the right), loop a band to connect the peg to the one above it. Repeat for three more pegs, connecting a column of four.

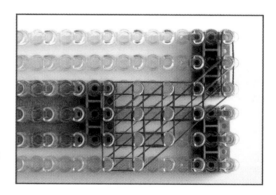

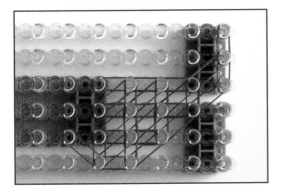

15. From the same bottom peg, attach a rubber band and connect it to the peg up one row and to the left.

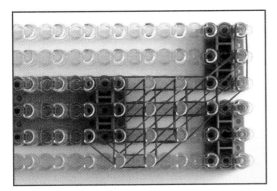

16. Start with the peg just above where you started your last band. Loop a rubber band over the peg and connect it to the peg to the left. Do the same for the next two pegs above the first.

17. Loop a rubber band around the top peg of your four-peg column (five pegs from the left and four from the bottom), and attach the other end diagonally to the peg one down and to the left. Do the same for the next peg down in the column.

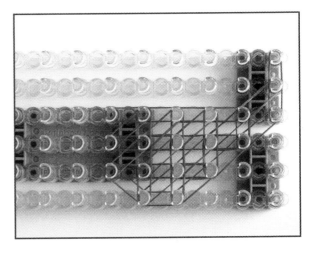

18. Start at the peg where you ended your last diagonal loop (six pegs from the left and one peg away from you). Loop a rubber band over the peg and connect it to the peg above it. Repeat this for the next peg up, making a column of three connected pegs.

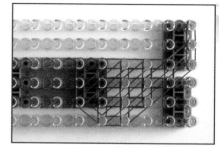

19. Loop a band around the top peg in your three-peg column, and connect the other end diagonally to the peg one down and to the left. Loop a band around the next peg down in the column, and attach it to the same peg to the left. Then loop a third rubber band to the bottom peg in the column, and connect it to the same peg up and to the left.

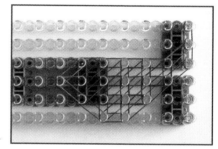

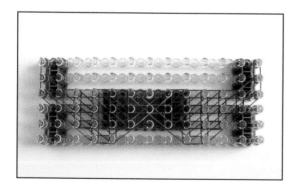

20. To make the other half of the mustache, repeat steps 2 through 19, but lead from the top left peg and move right.

21. When you have finished the other side of the mustache, take another rubber band and wrap it around the center peg three times.

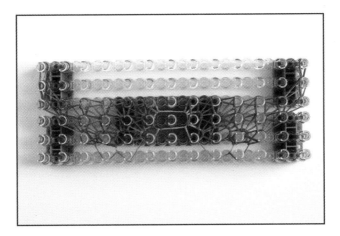

22. Start looping from the center and move outward to each end, pulling the bands off each peg, starting with the band on the bottom, and looping them back to the peg where it started. Loop the lower pegs first, and then work to the top. (This will be different than normal looping as the left side of the mustache will be looped in the opposite direction than normal.)

23. Once the entire mustache has been laid out, place a c-clip on both ends of the mustache.

24. To remove the mustache from the loom, begin pulling from both of the c-clips and work inward toward the center cap band.

Notes: To rock out your 'stache, you can tie a string to each end and wear it around your head. Alternatively, you can try skin-safe adhesive or double-sided sticky tape.

POOF BALL
SLiNG SHOT

Ready, aim, fire! This slingshot project is quick and easy—make a bunch with your friends, then line up and see who can shoot the farthest!

1. Set up the loom with three rows of pegs lined up squarely. Turn the loom so the arrow is facing away from you. Loop a band around the bottom left peg, and connect it to the peg above it. Continue to double loop up the left side of the loom, ending on the fifth peg from you. Do the same on the right side of the loom.

2. Loop a band around the middle fifth peg (right between your columns) and connect it to the peg below and to the left. Loop a second band around the middle peg and connect it to the peg below and to the right. Loop a band to the left peg in the fifth row, then connect it to the center peg in the row. Connect the center peg to the peg on the right.

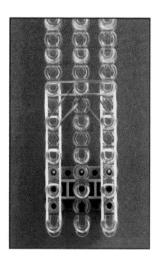

3. Connect the left peg in the fifth row to the peg above it. Do the same on the right side. Loop another band around the fifth peg on the left, and connect to the middle peg in the sixth row, up and to the right. Loop a band around the middle peg in the fifth row, and connect this to the middle peg in the sixth row. Connect the fifth peg on the right in the same way.

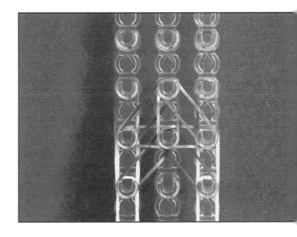

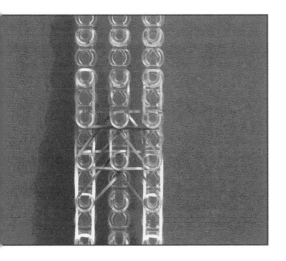

4. Loop a band around the sixth peg on the left and connect it to the middle peg in the row. Connect the middle peg to the peg on the right. Loop another band on the sixth peg on the left, and connect it to the peg above. Connect the middle peg in the sixth row to the peg above it. Connect the sixth peg on the right to the peg above it.

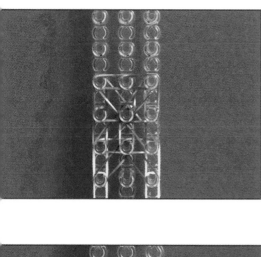

5. Loop a band around the middle peg in the sixth row, and connect it to the next peg up and to the left. Loop another band around the middle peg, and connect it up and to the right. Loop a band over the seventh peg on the left, and connect it to the next peg to the right. Repeat to connect the middle peg to the peg on the right.

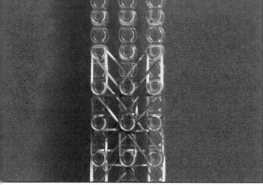

6. Connect the seventh peg on the left to the next peg above it. Do the same on the right side. Loop a band around the middle peg in the seventh row, and connect it to the peg up and to the left. Loop another band around the middle peg and connect it up and to the right.

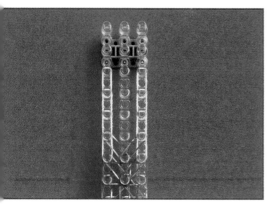

7. Starting on the eighth peg from you on the left, loop a band around the peg, and connect it to the peg above it. Repeat twice more to make a column of three bands. Do the same on the right side of the loom.

8. Turn your loom around so the arrow points
   toward you. Starting with the fourth peg
   from you on the left, hook the second band
   on the peg and pull it up and off, looping it
   back onto the peg where it started. Do the
   same with the next three pegs, then repeat
   on the right. Then loop the diagonal bands
   in the seventh row back onto the center
   peg. In the next two rows, loop the diagonal
   bands onto the center pegs, the horizontal
   bands from left to right, and then the vertical
   bands from the bottom to the top. Loop the

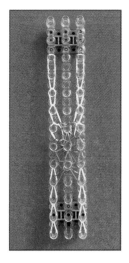

bands on the center peg back to the pegs they came from. Start
with the highest non-looped band, then work down until all
bands are looped. In this same row, loop the bands on the right
and left pegs to the pegs above them. From the center peg in the
next row, loop all non-looped bands back to the peg they started
on. Starting on the right and left in this same row, loop the
bands back up to the peg above it. Continue looping the right
and left columns in the same way until you reach the other end
of the loom.

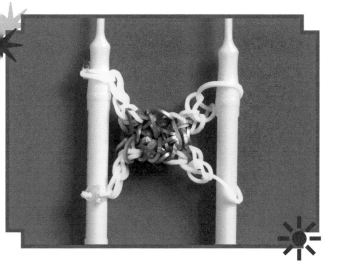

9. Remove
   your sling
   shot from
   the loom.

WATCH BAND

W ho wears a watch anymore? You do, with this cool watch band project!

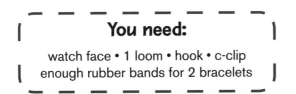

You need:

watch face • 1 loom • hook • c-clip
enough rubber bands for 2 bracelets

1. Set up your loom with the arrow pointing away from you.

2. Hook your favorite pattern onto the loom. We've used the straightaway pattern in our example. If your pattern has a cap band or an extra band at the end to hold it together, skip that step. Do not loop your project yet.

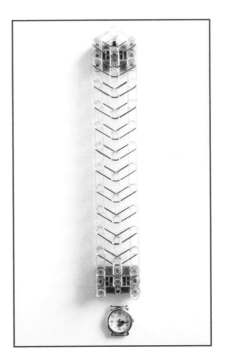

3. Turn the loom so the arrow is pointing toward you.

4. Take the bands at the beginning of the loom (the bands that were placed down last), thread them through the strap bars on the watch face, and loop them back to where they started.

5. Loop the rest of your loom following the directions for the pattern you used.

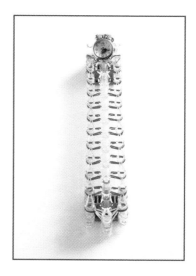

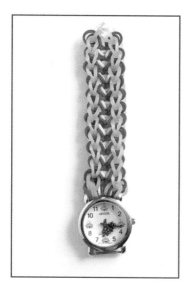

6. Attach a c-clip to the end, and remove the band from the loom.

7. Repeat steps 2 through 5 to make the other half of the watch band.

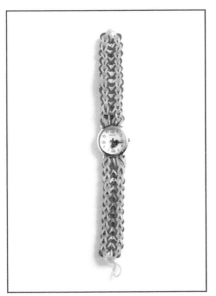

8. At the end of the second half of the watch band, run a rubber band through all the final loops and loop it back onto itself (like a lanyard knot). Remove it from the loom.

9. Hook the band to the c-clip, and enjoy your new watch!

DAiSY CHAIN
BRACELET

Add a little flower power to your loom magic! Create a delightful bracelet with a bouquet of your favorite flowers to wear on your wrist or ankle or even to loop as a key chain. This lovely daisy design is fashionable and fun for any occasion!

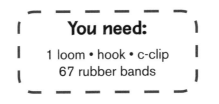

You need:

1 loom • hook • c-clip
67 rubber bands

1. Set up your loom with the middle pegs pulled one closer to you and the arrow pointing away from you. Loop a band around the first middle peg and connect it to the peg above it. Starting at the second middle peg, loop your bands to the left to make the first half of a hexagon, finishing on the fourth middle peg. Start again on the second middle peg, and loop your bands to the right in the same way to finish off your hexagon.

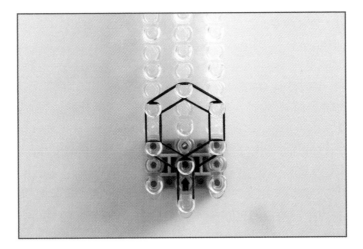

2. To make your "petals," loop a band around the third middle peg (in the center of your hexagon), and connect it to the peg up and to the right. Loop another band around the middle peg, and connect it to the peg down and to the right. Continue to connect all six of the outer pegs in this way, moving clockwise around the hexagon.

3. Triple-loop a band, and put it on the middle peg of your hexagon.

4. Starting on the last middle peg of your hexagon, repeat your pattern: loop both sides of a new hexagon, then add the bands from the center, and finish with a triple-looped cap band on the middle peg. Repeat this up the loom until you have five hexagons total. On the final hexagon, before you lay down your bands, loop a band around the last middle peg in the pattern and connect it to the last peg in the middle row, then complete the final flower pattern.

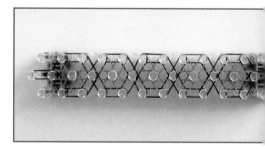

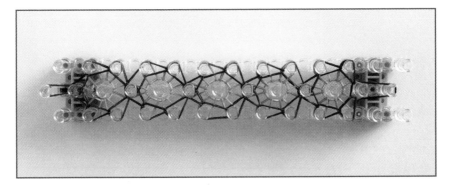

5. Turn the loom around so the arrow is facing toward you. Start looping the bands of your "petals" back onto the pegs where they started: First, loop the bands from the center of the hexagon, starting with the first band under the cap band, then loop counterclockwise around your hexagon. Next, loop the bands that make up the hexagon, starting from the left half and then the right in the same way you placed the bands there in the very first step. Loop all of the "flowers" this way, making your way to the end of the loom.

6. Loop the last band back to the last remaining peg. Attach a c-clip to secure the last band, and then remove your project from the loom.

7. For added length, loop more rubber bands through the end bands before attaching the c-clip.

RAiNBOW CHARM

This rainbow charm will brighten up your day! Whether you hang it from a window, glue it to a refrigerator magnet, or just have it as a keepsake, this eye-popping rainbow is sure to add a little color to your day—rain or shine!

You need:

2 looms • hook • c-clip • 13 PURPLE
26 BLUE • 26 GREEN • 26 • 26 ORANGE
and 27 RED rubber bands

1. Set up your two looms side by side with the arrows pointing right.

2. Starting at the bottom left-hand corner, double-loop an entire row of purple bands across the bottom row of the loom. To "double-loop," twist the band onto itself to create a double rubber band before stretching it onto the loom.

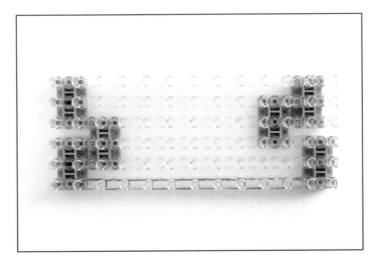

3. Loop a blue band around the peg in the bottom left corner, and then attach it to the next peg above. Do the same with the rest of the pegs in the first row.

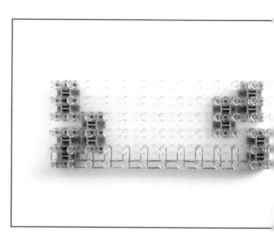

4. In the second row, attach a blue band to the peg all the way to the left, and then connect it to the next peg to the right. Continue looping from left to right until you reach the end of the row.

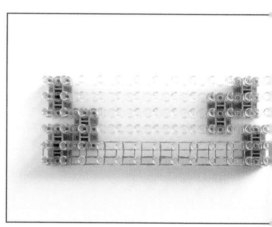

5. Repeat steps 3 and 4, first with green bands, then yellow, orange, and finally red.

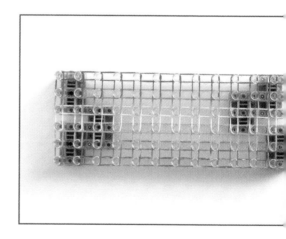

6. Triple-loop a band and put it onto the peg on the top right.

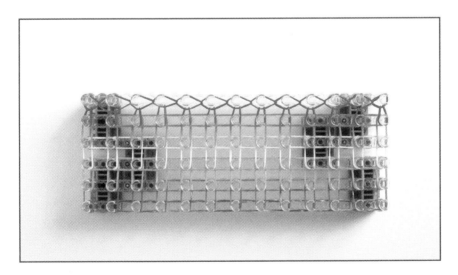

7. Begin looping your project by hooking the second band on the peg and pulling it up and off, then looping it back onto the peg where it started. First loop the top row from right to left, and then loop the vertical bands.

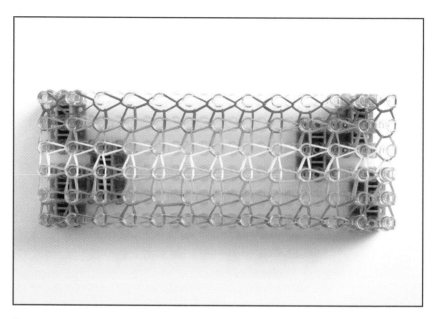

8. Repeat this process for each row.

9. Attach a c-clip to the band on the lower left.

10. Remove your completed project from your loom and see the beautiful rainbow!

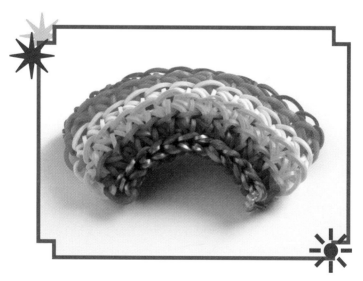

MATCHING BARRETTES

This pattern is a lot like the Octo-Bracelet pattern, but this time there are beads and barrettes to add a little extra fun! Make a matching set and wear them both, or give one to a friend!

You need:

1 loom • hook • 6 pony beads
2 craft barrettes • 25 rubber bands

1. Set up the loom with the middle pegs pulled one closer to you and the arrow pointing away from you. Loop a rubber band over the first middle peg, and then connect it to the peg up and to the left. Loop another band around this peg and connect it to the peg above it. Loop one band around the peg you ended on, and connect it to the third middle peg. Start at the middle peg closest to you and loop the right side of the circle in the same way.

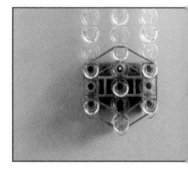

2. Thread a band through one of your beads. Hook one end of the band over the closest middle peg and the other around the middle peg of the circle. Thread a band through another bead, and connect the middle peg to the next peg in the row.

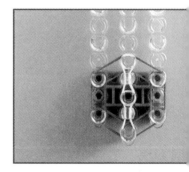

3. Repeat your circle pattern twice more, starting your new circle on the middle peg where you ended your last one, and adding the two beaded bands across the middle row like before. You should have three circles on your loom.

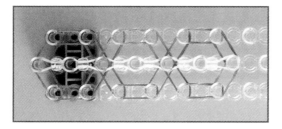

4. Hook a band around the last middle peg of your last circle and connect it to the peg above it.

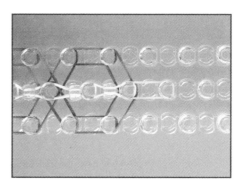

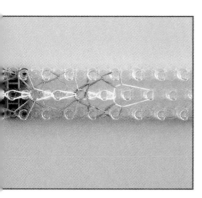

5. Turn the loom around so the arrow is pointing toward you. Starting at the top of your circle, hook the second band on the peg, pull it up and off the peg, and loop it back onto the peg where it began. Continue until all the bands on the peg are unlooped, and then continue looping the rest of the loom, moving toward the end until you have unlooped all the pegs.

6. Take a band and carefully loop it around the bands remaining on the last peg on the loom. Thread the band through its loop (like a lanyard hitch) and pull it tight. Pull it off the loom.

7. Thread one of your end bands through the metal hole of your barrette, and then pull the loop over the rest of the project to secure it. Thread the other end band through the other hole and tie it tightly.

8. Repeat for the other barrette.

CELLPHONE CASE

Dress up your phone with your own custom-made case! This project stretches to fit, so you do not have to worry about measuring. Try out different color combinations and patterns; you can even make a different case for every day of the week!

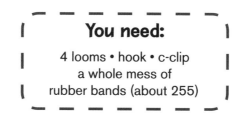

You need:

4 looms • hook • c-clip
a whole mess of
rubber bands (about 255)

1. Connect your four looms side by side with the pegs lined up square and the arrows pointing away from you.

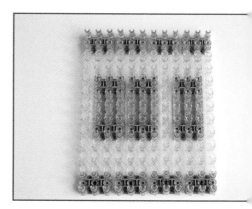

2. Loop a band around one of the middle pegs in the row closest to you, and connect it to the peg right above it.

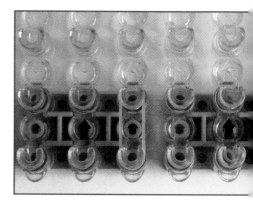

3. Double-loop a rubber band around the peg where you ended your last band, and connect it to the peg to the right. Continue to double-loop to the right for five total pegs, ending on the second to last peg on the right. Then start again at the second middle peg, and loop five more bands in the same way, moving to the left and ending on the last peg in the row.

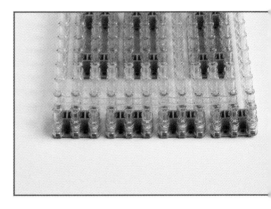

3a. Starting on the corner pegs where you ended your last row, double-loop all the way to the top of the loom on both sides.

3b. Double-loop the top row, starting at the ends of the columns you just made and working toward the middle from both sides of the row, ending on the middle peg.

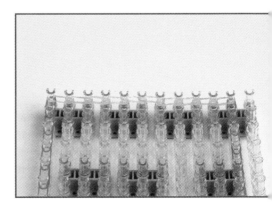

4. Loop a band on the second peg in the second row of your loom, and connect it to the peg above it. Repeat this for the rest of the pegs in the second row, ending on the peg before the right side of your rectangle.

5. Loop a rubber band around the third middle peg, then around the next peg to the right. Repeat for five total pegs. Start again at the third middle peg, and loop five more bands in the same way, moving to the left and ending on the last peg in the row.

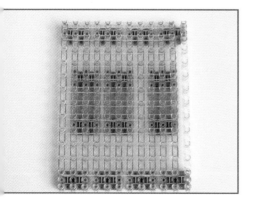

6. Repeat this pattern all the way up the rest of the loom, looping up from your last row, then looping across the pegs where you ended your loops, moving out from the center peg in the row. When you reach the second to last row on the loom, stop after you loop your row moving out from the center, and don't loop bands up to the final row.

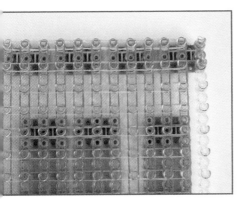

7. Start at the second peg in the top row, and connect it to the peg below it. Move to the next peg to the right and do the same. Continue across the top row of your rectangle, like you did along the bottom earlier.

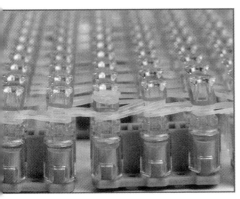

8. Triple-loop a band, and then slide it onto the middle peg in the top row.

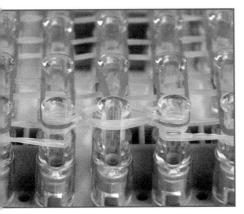

9. Rotate the loom so the arrows are pointed away from you.

10. On the middle peg where you put your triple-looped band, hook the second band and lift it up and off, looping it back onto the peg where the other end is hooked. Repeat this for the next band on the peg and again for the last one.

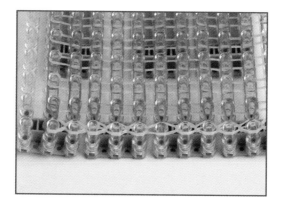

11. Move to the next peg to the left and repeat the process, starting with the second rubber band and looping each band back onto the peg where it started. Do the same with all of the pegs in the row, finishing the pegs on the left, then repeating the process with the pegs to the right of the center peg.

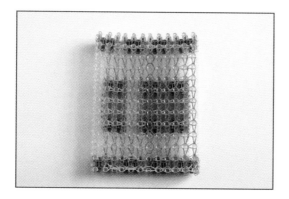

12. Starting at the middle peg in the next row up, repeat the unlooping process, hooking the second band on the peg and looping it back onto the peg where it began. Continue to loop the rest of the rows inside your rectangle in the same way, moving up the loom row by row and working your way from the middle peg, first to the left, then to the right. Do not do the last row yet.

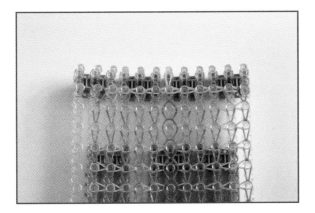

13. On the last row, start at the peg at the top left corner of your rectangle. Hook the second rubber band on the peg and pull it up and off the peg, looping it onto the peg to the right. Continue looping like this until you get to the middle peg, and then do the same starting at the corner peg on the right.

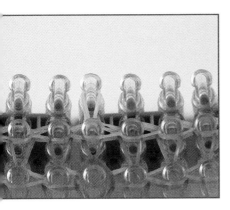

14. When you reach the middle peg, grab the bottom rubber band with your hook and pull it up and off the peg and back to the peg above it.

15. Secure the loops on this last peg with a c-clip.

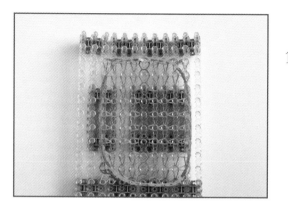

16. Remove your project from the loom, starting with the tightest edge, and then pull the rest off the loom.

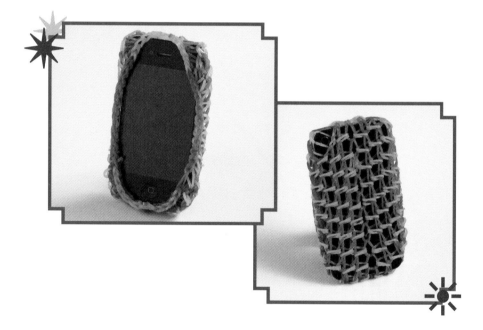

Now just stretch the case over the back of your phone, and you are good to go! If the case is too big, you can try again with three looms instead of four; just be sure you always have an odd number of columns or the case will come unraveled.

CANDY CANE ORNAMENT

Create a festive candy cane ornament to celebrate the holiday season! This simple project is decorative and fun, but it definitely will not taste like peppermint stick, so try not to eat it when you are done!

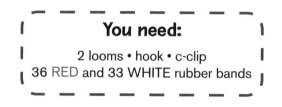

You need:

2 looms • hook • c-clip
36 RED and 33 WHITE rubber bands

1. Set up your looms beside each other with the arrows pointing away from you. Flip the two columns on the right so the arrows are pointing toward you. Loop a white band around the peg at the bottom left corner, and connect it to the peg to the right. Loop another white band around the corner peg, and connect it to the next peg above it.

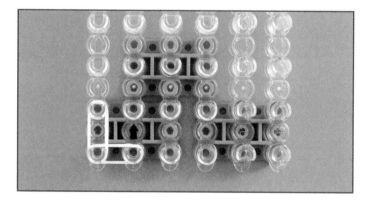

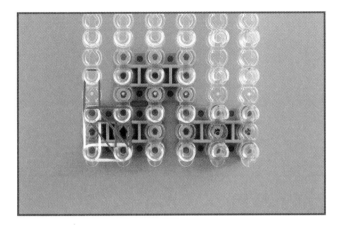

2. Loop a red band around the second peg in the bottom row, and connect it to the peg above it. Loop a red band around that peg, and connect it to the peg to the left. Loop another red band around the second peg in the first row, and connect it up and to the left. Loop another red band around the second peg in the first column, and connect it to the peg above it.

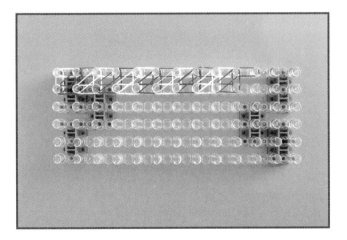

3. Starting on the second peg in the second row, repeat step 2, using white bands. Continue to repeat step 2 in this way, alternating red and white bands, with your last band ending on the third peg from the end of the loom.

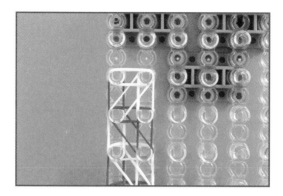

4. Loop a white band over the fourth peg from the end in the second column, and connect it to the peg above it. Loop another white band over the fourth band from the end in the first column, and connect it to the peg up and to the right. Loop one white band over the third peg from the end in the first column, and connect it to the peg to the right.

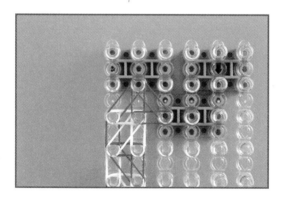

5. Loop a red band around the third peg from the top in the first column, and connect it to the peg up and to the right. Loop a red band around the third peg from the end in the second column, and connect it to the peg above; then loop another band around the same peg, and connect it to the peg to the right. Loop a red band around the peg where you just ended your loop, and connect it to the peg up and to the left.

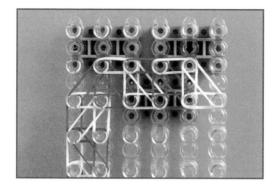

6. Loop a white band around the peg at the top of your last red triangle, and connect it to the peg to the right. Loop a white band around the peg where you ended your loop, and connect it to the next peg down. From that peg, loop another white band to the next peg on the right, then loop a white band around that peg and connect it to the peg up and to the left, where you started your triangle. Repeat twice more, alternating colors.

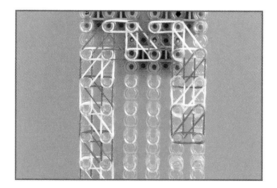

7. Loop a red band around the third peg down in the second to last row, and connect it to the peg below. Do the same with the third peg in the last column. Loop a red band around the fourth peg from the end in the second to last column, and connect it to the peg up and to the right. Loop another band on the same peg, and connect it to the right. Repeat this pattern twice more, starting at the next row down and alternating colors. Double loop your last red band.

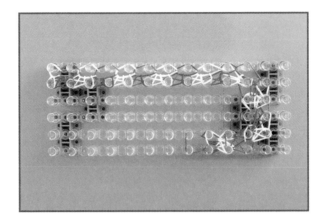

8. Start at the pegs you just double-looped. Hook the second band on the peg and loop it back to the peg where it started. Loop the rest of the project in this way, working your way back to the beginning of the candy cane.

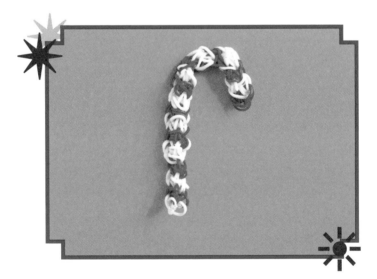

9. After you remove the candy cane from the looms, you can fit a hook into the top of the cane to make decorating simple!

PEACE SiGN

Peace, love, and magic looms! This far-out peace sign comes together quickly and looks cool hanging in your window or on your wall!

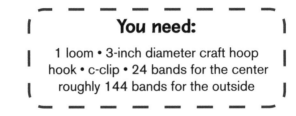
1. Set up the loom with the middle column set one peg closer to you and with the arrow pointing away from you. Loop a band around the first middle peg, and connect it to the next peg above it. Repeat until you reach the end of the loom.

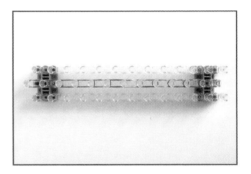

2. Loop a band around the first peg on the left, and connect it to the next peg above it. Repeat for five total bands. Do the same on the right side.

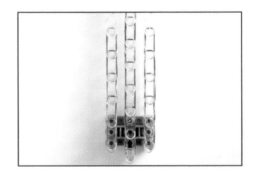

3. Loop a band around the sixth peg on the left side, and connect it to the peg up one and to the right. Loop a band around the sixth peg on the right, and connect it to the same middle peg.

4. Turn the loom around and, starting with the peg closest to you, pull the second band on each peg up and off, looping it back onto the peg where the other end is looped. Continue until you reach the end of the loom.

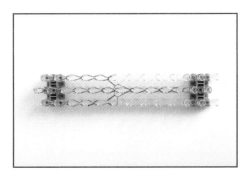

5. Pull your bands from the loom, and stretch them over your craft hoop.

6. Turn your loom so the arrow is pointing away from you. Loop a band around the first middle peg, and connect it to the peg up and to the left. Loop a band around the peg you ended on and connect it up and to the right. Continue this zigzag pattern until you reach the end of the loom.

7. Lay your craft hoop over your zigzag pattern. Starting at the second looped peg on the end, hook the second band on the peg and pull it up and off, looping it over the craft hoop and back onto the peg where the other end of the band is looped. Continue looping in this way all the way down the loom. As the bands are looped, pull them from the loom. Use a c-clip to secure the final band, or leave your hook on the loop to keep it from unraveling. Lay out your zigzag pattern again. Remove the c-clip from the band on the craft hoop and slide both ends of the band onto the top middle peg of your zigzag. Starting on this peg, loop the bands on your loom over the craft hoop and back onto their starting pegs as you did before.

8. Repeat steps 6 and 7 until you have covered your craft hoop. Secure the final loop with a c-clip, then connect it to the starting loop on the loom.

BLOOMING BEADED BRACELET

Take the Daisy Chain Bracelet and jazz it up! This neat bouquet of a bracelet adds cool beads to the "flowers," making it extra special and beautiful! Whether you like pretty pinks and blues or prefer the colors of your favorite sports team and beads that look like soccer balls or footballs, mix and match to make it your own!

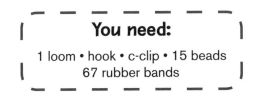

You need:

1 loom • hook • c-clip • 15 beads
67 rubber bands

1. Set up your loom with the middle pegs pulled one closer to you and the arrow pointing away from you. Loop a band around the first middle peg, and connect it to the peg above it. Starting at the second middle peg, loop your bands to the left to make the first half of a hexagon, finishing on the fourth middle peg. Start again on the second middle peg, and loop your bands to the right in the same way to finish off your hexagon.

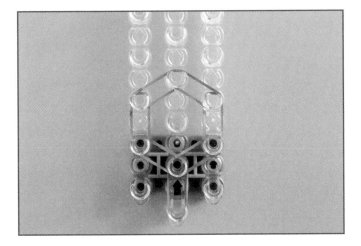

2. To make your "petals," loop a band around the third middle peg (in the center of your hexagon), and connect it to the peg up and to the right. Thread the *second* rubber band "petal" through a bead, then loop another band around the middle peg, and connect it to the peg down and to the right. Continue to connect all six of the outer pegs in this way, moving clockwise around the hexagon and switching off with a bead every other band.

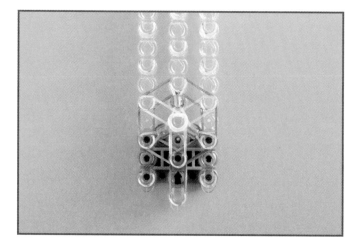

3. Triple-loop a band and put it on the middle peg of your hexagon.

4. Starting on the last middle peg of your hexagon, repeat your pattern: loop both sides of a new hexagon, then add the bands from the center. With the second "flower," add the bead on the *first* "petal," and then trade off beading every other petal. Finish with a triple-looped cap band on the middle peg. Repeat this up the loom until you have five hexagons total, trading off between placing the beads on the first and second "petals." On the final hexagon, before you lay down your bands, loop a band

around the last middle peg in the pattern and connect it to the last peg in the middle row, then complete the final flower pattern.

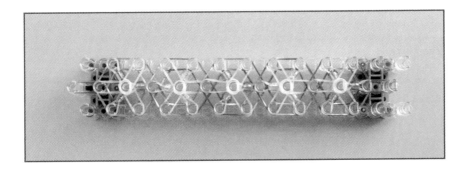

5. Turn the loom around so the arrow is facing toward you. Start looping the bands of your "petals" back onto the pegs where they started: First, loop the bands from the center of the hexagon, starting with the first band under the cap band, then loop counterclockwise around your hexagon. Next, loop the bands that make up the hexagon, starting from the left half and then the right in the same way you placed the bands in the very first step. Loop all of the "flowers" this way, making your way to the end of the loom.

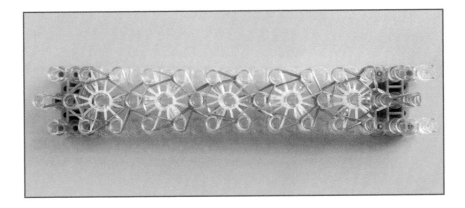

6. Loop the last band back to the remaining peg. Attach a c-clip to secure the last band, and then remove your project from the loom.

7. For added length, loop more rubber bands through the end bands before attaching the c-clip.

SPORTS FAN
KEY CHAIN

Show your team pride or school spirit with this customizable key chain! The stretchy loop slips over your wrist so you'll never lose your keys, even while you cheer your team on!

You need:

2 looms • hook • key clip • c-clip several beads • 27 bands for the loop • 38 bands for the keychain

1. Set up your looms end to end with the pegs square and the arrow pointing away from you. Remove the center pegs. Loop a band over the bottom left peg, and connect it to the third peg up.

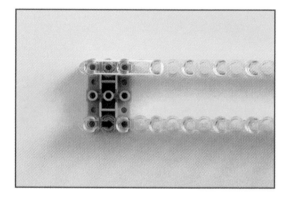

2. Move to the second peg in the column, and connect it to the third peg above it. Repeat all the way up the loom. Do the same on the right side.

3a. Loop a band around the second peg from the end in the left column. Connect it to the peg above it. Do the same on the right side.

3b. Double-loop a band and connect it to both end pegs.

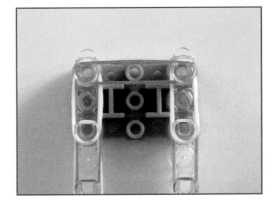

4. Turn your loom so the arrow points toward you. Starting with the pegs closest to you, hook the second band on the peg and pull it up and off, looping it back to the peg where it started.

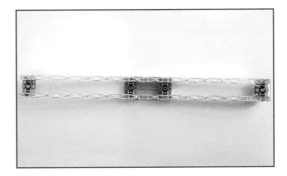

5. Secure the end loops with a c-clip or your hook for now. Pull the project off the loom.

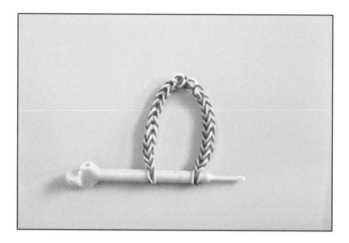

6. Set up a single loom with the pegs offset, with middle pegs closer to you and with the arrow pointing away from you. Starting on the first middle peg, loop a band around the peg, and connect it to the next peg up and to the left. Loop a band around that peg, and connect it to the next peg up in the row. Continue looping this way to the end of the loom, ending your last loop on the last middle peg. Start again at the first middle peg, and do the same for the right side.

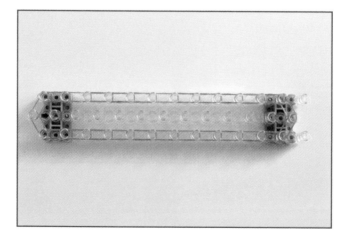

7. Loop a band around the first peg on the left, and connect it to the first peg on the right. Repeat until you reach the end of the loom. To add beads, thread the band through the bead before putting it on the loom. Letter beads should go in the order shown, with the words starting at the opposite end from where you started laying out the project.

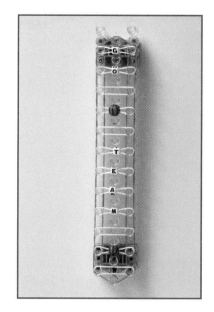

8. Attach the first half of your project to your loom, sliding all of the loops onto the peg above your first letter bead.

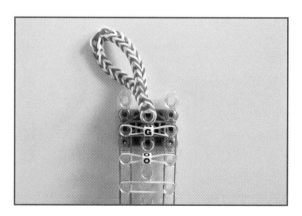

9. Starting with that same top middle peg, hook the band below the bands you just added, and pull it off the peg, looping it back onto the peg where it started. Loop both bands off this first middle peg, then loop the rest of the project the same way, working towards the other end of the loom.

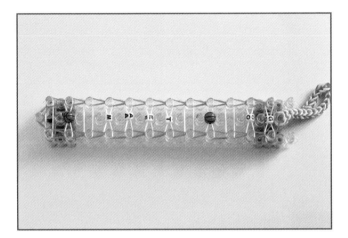

10. Secure the final loops with a c-clip and attach a key clip.

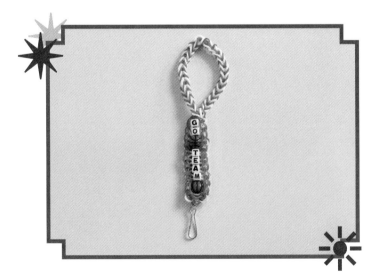

RAiNBOW RiNG

Show off your rubber band skills with this impressive piece of bling! Use brightly colored beads to make this ring really pop, or make like the big leagues and use sports beads for a championship ring!

You need:

1 loom • hook • c-clip
11 beads • 23 rubber bands

1. Set up your loom with the middle pegs closer to you and the arrow pointing away. Loop a band around the peg closest to you, and then connect it to the peg above it. Loop a band around the second middle peg, and connect it to the peg up and to the right. Loop another band around the second middle peg, and connect it up and to the left. Loop two bands up on either side of the loom. Loop a band around the fifth peg in the middle column, and connect it to the peg above it. Then loop a band around the fourth peg in the right column, and connect it to the peg where you ended your last loop. Do the same on the left.

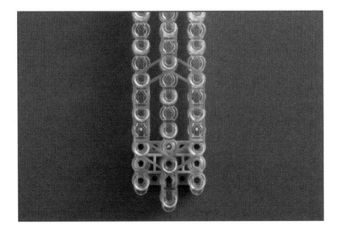

2. To add your beads, thread a band through a bead and loop one end around the first middle peg in your hexagon. Connect the other end of the band up and to the right, then repeat with the rest of the pegs as shown, moving clockwise until you have looped five beaded bands.

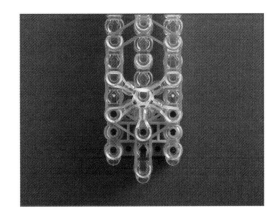

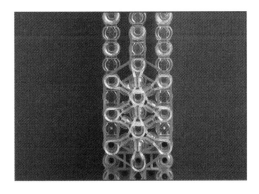

3. Repeat step 2 on the next middle peg in your hexagon. Loop your first beaded band to the peg up and to the right, then loop the rest of the pegs around the middle peg, moving clockwise. This time you will connect a band to the middle peg below.

4. Triple-loop a cap band onto both middle pegs in the hexagon.

5. Turn your loom so the arrow points toward you. Start with the triple-looped peg closest to you. Hook the first band under the cap band and pull it off, looping it back to the peg where it started, which should

be the peg directly beneath the middle peg. Continue looping around the circle this way, moving counterclockwise, until you have looped all the bands off the peg. Do the same with the next middle peg, looping the first band under the cap band off and back to where the other end of the band is looped, which should be the peg to the bottom right of the center peg. Continue looping the bands off the middle peg in this way, moving counterclockwise. When you have finished all the bands on the two middle pegs, loop the outside bands, starting with the three bands on the second middle peg closest to you and then working up both sides. Finish by looping the top middle peg.

6. Secure both loose ends with a c–clip. Fasten the two ends together to make your ring! If it is too tight, loop a few bands together and connect them to the c–clip to make it bigger.

PENCIL TOPPER

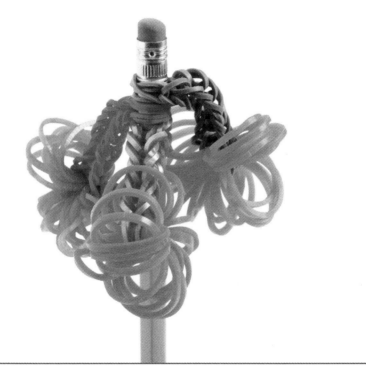

Make writing and drawing even more fun by giving your pencils some extra flare! This pencil topper is super easy to make and can fit over your pencils and pens or can be made into a key ring for even more loom entertainment!

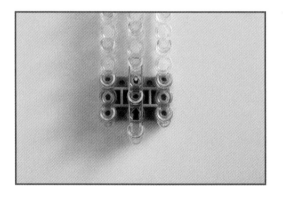

1. Start with the loom offset with the center pegs closer to you and the arrow pointing away. Loop a band over the first middle peg, and connect it to the third peg up.

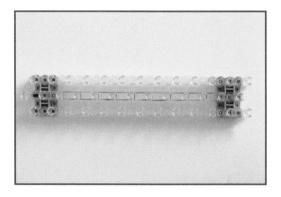

2. Loop a band around the next peg up, and connect it to the third peg above it. Continue looping the middle pegs this way all the way up the loom, until there is one empty peg left at the top of the loom.

3. Loop a band over the middle peg where you ended your last band, and connect it to the peg below it.

4. Loop a band around the second to last peg in the middle column, and connect it to the peg up and to the left. Loop another band around the second middle peg, and connect it to the next peg up. Loop another band around the second middle peg, and connect it to the next peg up and to the right.

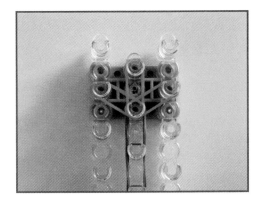

5. Repeat step 4 until you cannot fit any more bands on the peg. This example uses twenty-four total bands, eight for each peg.

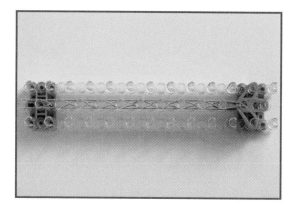

6. Starting at the second middle peg from the end (where you stacked all of the bands for the charm), loop the bottom band (the green band here) and pull it off the peg, looping it back onto the peg where it started. Continue looping this way as you work your way down the loom back to where you started.

7. Slide your pencil through the bands on the second peg, and then remove your project from the loom!

NUNCHUKS

Rubber bands meet martial arts! Nunchuks are an awesome tool used in karate and Okinawan kobudō, which are forms of Japanese martial arts. They help improve speed and hand movements in training, but they look really cool, too! These nunchuks are made mostly of rubber bands, but be careful—there is metal wire to keep them firm, so never use these in a way that might hurt someone. Try out this great project and have fun!

You need:
1 loom • hook • 2 c-clips
2 metal craft wires • 143 bands

1. Set up your loom with the pegs square and the arrow pointing away from you. Loop a band around the first center peg, and connect it to the peg to the left. Loop another band on the center peg, and connect it to the peg to the right. Loop a band around each peg in the first row, and connect the peg to the next one above it. Loop a band around the left peg in the first row, and connect it to the next middle peg. Do the same with the right peg in the first row.

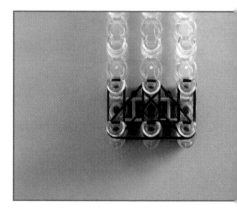

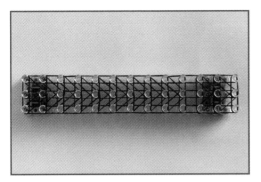

2. Repeat your pattern on each row of the loom until you reach the end.

3. Triple-loop a band over the center peg in the top row of the loom.

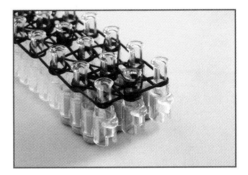

4. Lay your craft wire over your loom bent double, as shown, with the bent end resting above the top middle peg. Starting with the second band on the top middle peg, loop the bands up and off the peg and over the craft wire, hooking them back onto the peg

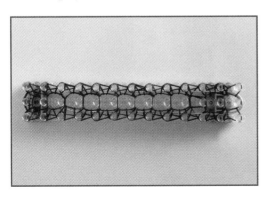

where the other end of the band is looped. After the center peg, loop the side pegs in the same way, then move to the next row and repeat. On the final row, loop the bands from the corner pegs onto the center peg.

5. Secure the loose bands with the c-clips, and remove your project from the loom. Repeat the steps to make a second nunchuk.

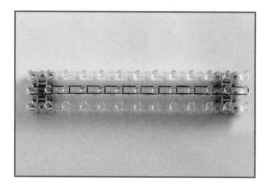

6. Loop a line of bands down the center of your loom. Turn the loom around, and loop the bands back onto the pegs where they started.

7. Remove the chain from the loom and attach either end to the c-clips of the nunchuks.

TRIPLE-OCTO SHOELACE CHARMS

Make your kicks twice as cool with these Triple-Octo Shoelace Charms! You can customize them with different beads and colors to suit your style.

You need:

1 loom • hook • c-clip • 7 beads (6 pony beads and 1 shaped bead) • 26 rubber bands

1. Set up your loom with the center pegs closer to you and the arrow pointing away from you. Starting on the center peg closest to you, do one Octo stitch: loop three bands around to make the left side of the hexagon, then start at the first center peg and do the same on the right side. Thread a band through a bead, and attach it to the first and second middle peg. Thread another band through a bead and attach it to the second and third middle pegs.

2. Starting on the middle peg where you ended your last Octo, do two more Octo stitches in the same way. Thread a band through a bead, attach the band to the top middle peg in your last Octo, and then connect it to the next peg above it. Loop a band around that peg, and connect it to the peg above it.

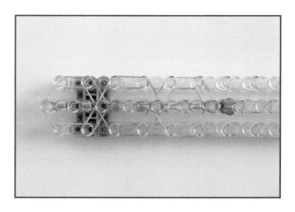

3. Turn the loom so the arrow points toward you. Starting with the looped pegs closest to you, loop the bands off the pegs and back onto the pegs where they began. Always hook the second unlooped band on the peg and loop it, looping all of the bands on a peg before moving on to the next peg. Loop all of the pegs in this way, working your way to the end of the loom.

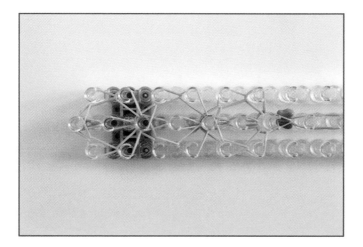

4. Secure the loose bands on the final peg with a c-clip or tie it off with another rubber band. Remove your charm from the loom.

5. Make two more Triple-Octo charms in the same way. Hook all the end loops together with a c-clip and attach to your shoelaces!

SPORTS BAND

Cheer on your team with this sports-themed band! Change up the beads and the colors to match your team's uniform—you can make a different one for all your favorite teams!

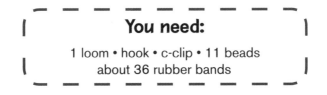

You need:

1 loom • hook • c-clip • 11 beads
about 36 rubber bands

1. Set up your loom with the middle pegs closer to you and the arrow pointing away from you. Loop a band around the first center peg, and connect it to the peg up and to the left. Do the same on the other side. Starting with the pegs where you ended your bands, loop a line of bands up both outside columns on the loom, looping the last bands onto the last middle peg.

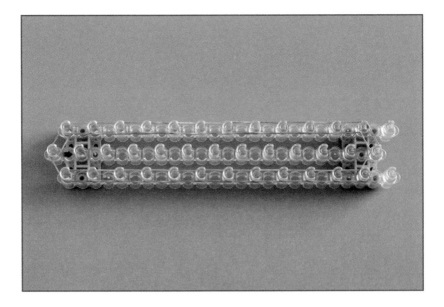

2. Thread a band through a sports bead, and loop it over the outside pegs in the second row. Continue up the loom in this way, stretching the beaded bands across the columns you created.

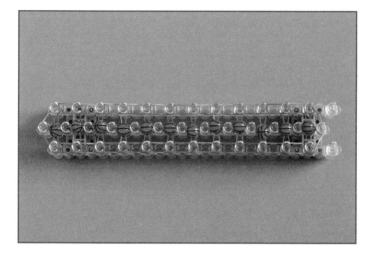

3. Triple-loop a band on the last middle peg.

4. Turn the loom so the arrow is pointing toward you. Hook the second band on the middle peg closest to you, and pull it off the peg, looping it back to the peg where it started. Loop all the bands off the closest middle peg this way, then loop the rest of the bands along the outside of the loom, working your way to the middle peg at the other end of the loom. Do not loop the beaded bands.

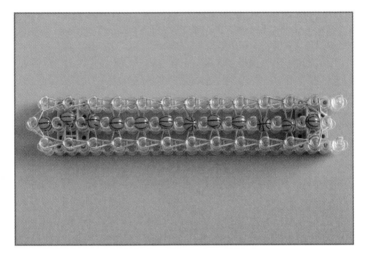

5. Secure the loops on the final peg with a rubber band or a c-clip. Remove your project from the loom.

PiNNACLe CHOKeR PENDANT

Jazz up your necklace by adding a gorgeous pendant! This extra step will take your jewelry from simple to sophisticated–choose your favorite color of the rainbow, or try using every color to continue the cool rainbow effect!

You need:

3 looms • hook • c-clip • 6 beads
15 rubber bands

To Make the Choker:

1. Set up three looms the long way, with the arrows pointing toward you. Lay out the pattern for the Pinnacle Bracelet [page 9], repeating until you reach the end of the third loom.

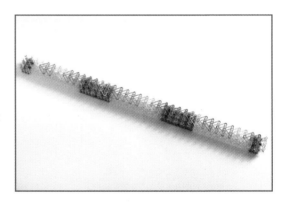

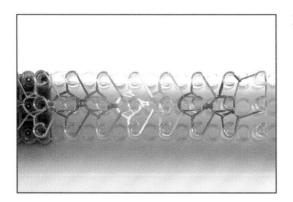

2. Loop the bands back to the pegs where they started, as usual, then secure the loose bands on the final peg with a c-clip.

Remove the choker from the loom and set aside.

To Make the Pendant:

1. Set up your loom
   with the middle
   pegs closer to you
   and the arrow
   pointing away
   from you. Loop a
   band around the
   first middle peg,
   and connect it
   to the peg above

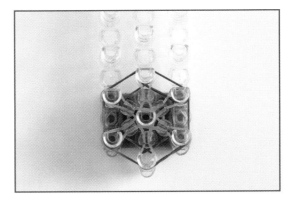

   it. Starting at the second middle peg, loop your bands to the
   left to make the first half of a hexagon, finishing on the fourth
   middle peg. Start again on the second middle peg, and loop
   your bands to the right in the same way to finish off your
   hexagon.

2. To make the spokes that will feature the beads, thread six
   bands with your six beads. With the first beaded band, loop it
   around the third middle peg (in the center of your hexagon),
   and connect it to the peg up and to the right. Continue to
   connect all six of the outer pegs with the beaded bands in
   this way, moving
   clockwise around
   the hexagon. Then,
   triple-loop a band
   on the middle peg
   of your hexagon as
   a cap band.

3. Triple-loop another band on the fourth middle peg (the top of your hexagon) as another cap band. Turn the loom around so the arrow is facing toward you. Start looping the bands of your spokes

back onto the pegs where they started: First, loop the bands from the center of the hexagon, starting with the first band under the cap band, then loop counterclockwise around your hexagon. Next, loop the outer bands, starting from the left half and then the right in the same way you placed the bands in the very first step.

4. Loop the last band back to the remaining peg. Attach a c-clip to secure the last band, and then remove your project from the loom. Attach the pendant to the middle of the choker, or make several pendants and line the whole thing!

SNOWMAN ORNAMENT

It's getting frosty out there! Get into the winter spirit by using this cool snowman as an ornament or decoration, attaching it to your backpack, or gluing it to a refrigerator magnet. Luckily, he won't melt!

You need:

3 looms • hook • c-clip • 20 clear or white bands

For the Snowman's Head:

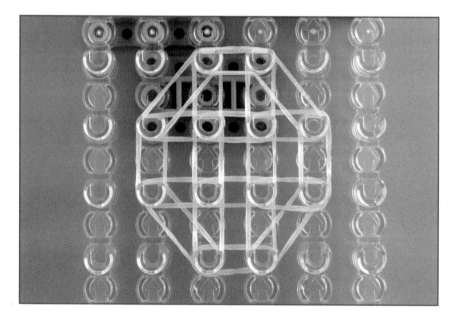

1. Connect two looms side by side with the arrow pointing away from you. Loop a band around the two middle pegs of the row. Loop bands around each of these pegs, and connect them to the pegs above them. Loop a band around the left middle peg, and connect it to the peg up and to the left. Loop a band around the right middle peg, and connect it to the peg up and to the right.

2. Loop a row of bands across the four pegs in the next row where you ended your last loops. Loop bands around each of these four pegs, and connect them to the peg above them.

3. Loop across the pegs where you ended your last loops again, moving from left to right. Connect the two middle bands in this row to the pegs above them.

4. Connect the outside pegs in this row up and diagonally toward the middle of the loom as shown. Double-loop a cap band around the top two pegs in the shape.

5. Starting at the top two pegs of the circle, loop the bands back onto the pegs where they started, first looping the second band on the peg, then working your way down the peg.

6. Hook your pattern in the opposite way you put it on the loom, hooking the loops down, then from right to left.

7. Secure the loose bands with a c-clip.

8. Remove your circle from the loom and put aside.

For the Snowman's Torso:

You need:

2 looms • hook • c-clip • 41 bands

1. Set up your looms side by side with the arrow pointing away from you, and repeat the pattern you did for the head circle, laying out the shape as shown. This will require more bands to make a larger circle.

2. Loop bands from right to left, then loop up to the next row, using diagonal loops to make your circle wider in the center, then smaller at the end.

3. Finish your pattern with a double-loop cap band across the top middle pegs. Hook your bands back onto the pegs where they started, beginning with the top middle pegs. Always hook the second unlooped band on the peg.

4. Loop all of the bands on a peg before moving to the next peg: loop down from the top row, then across from right to left, then repeat.

5. Secure the loose bands on the final pegs with a c-clip.

6. Remove your circle from the loom and set it aside.

For the Snowman's Base:

1. Set up your looms with two connected side by side, adding two additional columns.

2. Create your circle as you did with the smaller circles, laying the shape out as shown. Don't forget to secure the pattern with a double-loop cap band across the top middle pegs.

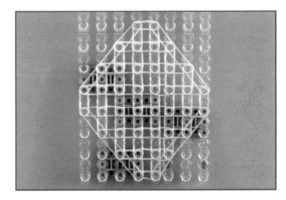

3. Hook the bands back as you did before.

4. Secure the loose bands on the final pegs and remove your circle from the loom.

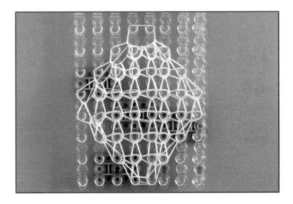

To Assemble Your Snowman:

1. Connect your three circles with the c-clips, as shown.

2. Double loop a band around the head and body circles to make a scarf.

3. Knot two brown bands together, loop the end through the body circle, and pull the other end of the band through the loop to secure it. Do the same for the other arm.

4. Add the face and buttons by pulling bands through the project from the back, leaving the loose ends in the back.

ROCKER CUFF BRACELET

Rock and roll with this awesome, stylish cuff bracelet! Make a cuff with all one color, or make a whole rainbow to go up your arm!

1. Set up your four looms side by side, with the arrows pointing right. Starting at the bottom left-hand corner, loop dark green bands across the bottom row of the loom, looping from left to right. Loop a dark green band around the peg in the bottom left corner, and then attach it to the next peg above. Do the same with the rest of the pegs in the first row. Loop across the second row with the dark green bands again, going from left to right.

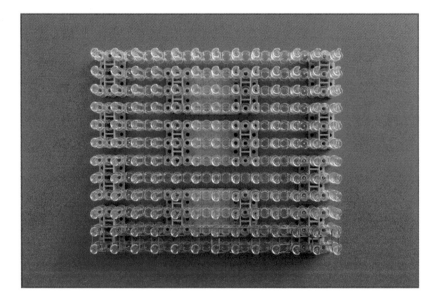

2. Loop another set of dark green bands coming up from this row as you did before. Then loop across the third row in your next color (light green), looping left to right. Repeat this process all the way up the

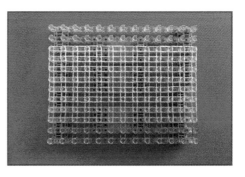

loom, looping across a row, up, across, and up once more before switching to the next color. For the white bands, repeat the same process, but you will not need a final row of vertical loops.

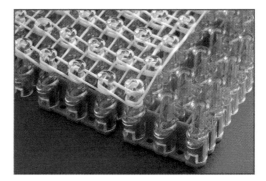

3. Triple-loop a cap band and put it onto the peg on the top right (which will be a white band).

4. Starting with the peg with the cap band, begin looping your project by hooking the band right below the cap band, pulling it up and off the peg, and looping it back onto the peg where it started. First loop the top row from right to left, and then loop the vertical bands. Repeat this process for each row.

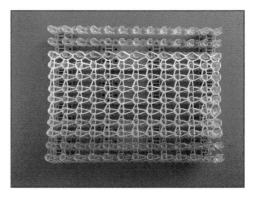

5. Attach a c-clip to the band on the lower left. Remove the first half of your cuff from the loom.

6. Repeat these steps for the second half of your cuff. Once you have both sides of your cuff, attach them together by looping a band through the end of the cuff with the corresponding end of the other side. Do this with five bands, one for each color in the cuff. Attach these bands to c-clips to secure. Now you have a great, stylish cuff!

BLiNG RiNG

Don't settle for a plain ring; go big and make a bling ring! This beautiful piece of jewelry combines a ring and a bracelet—it's fit for a fashionista!

To Make the Stone:

1. Set up your loom with the middle pegs pulled closer to you and the arrow pointing away from you. Loop a band around the first middle peg, and connect it to the peg above it. Loop a band around the fourth middle peg, and connect it to the peg above it. Starting at the second middle peg, loop your bands to the left to make the first half of a hexagon, finishing on the fourth middle peg. Start again on the second middle peg, and loop your bands to the right in the same way to finish off your hexagon.

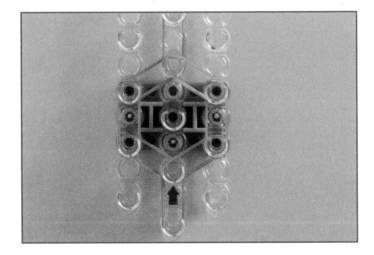

2. To make the spokes that will feature the beads, thread six bands with your six beads. With the first beaded band, loop it around the third middle peg (in the center of your hexagon), and connect it to the peg up and to the right. Continue to connect all six of the outer pegs with the beaded bands in this

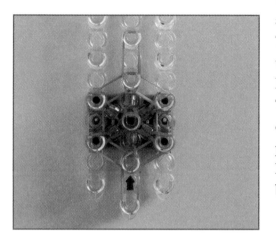

way, moving clockwise around the hexagon. Triple-loop a band on the middle peg of your hexagon as a cap band. Triple-loop another band on the fourth middle peg (the top of your hexagon) as another cap band.

3. Turn the loom around so the arrow is facing toward you. Start looping the bands of your spokes back onto the pegs where they started: First, loop the bands from the center of the hexagon, starting with the first band under the cap band, then loop counterclockwise around your hexagon. Next, loop the outer bands, starting from the left half and then the right in the same way that you placed the bands in the very first step.

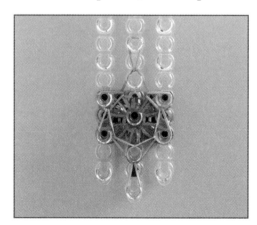

4. Loop the last band back to the last remaining peg. Attach a c-clip to secure the loose bands on either end, and then remove your project from the loom. Connect the c-clipped bands to make your ring band: loop several bands through one another to extend the band if it is too small.

To Make the Bracelet:

You need:

1 loom • hook
c-clip • 50 bands

1. Lay your loom horizontally with the arrow pointing to your right. Move the middle row all the way down and attach it to the loom on the second-to-last peg, so that it looks like a big

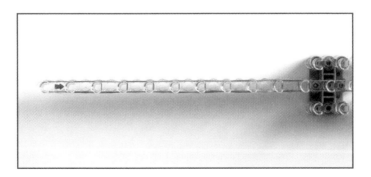

letter Y. Starting with the bottom of the Y, loop your first color
from the first peg to the third peg (skipping the second peg).
Loop your second color from the second peg to the fourth
peg (skipping the third peg). Loop your third color from the
third peg to the fifth peg (skipping the fourth peg). Repeat this
pattern until you have reached the end of the row.

2. Now that you are at the base of the loom, loop a band from
the second middle peg (the one that is next to last in the row)
around the peg above it *and* the peg up and to the left of that
peg (it will be the third peg in the first row). The loop will
appear triangular. Loop another band from the same middle peg
around the one above it and the one up and to the right (the
third peg in the third row). The loop will appear triangular in
the opposite direction. From the last peg in the middle row, loop
a band around the peg up and to the left *and* the peg just above
that one (the fourth peg in the first row). This loop will also
appear triangular. From the last peg in the middle row, loop a
band around the peg up and to the right *and* the peg just above
that one as well (the fourth peg in the third row). This loop will
appear triangular.

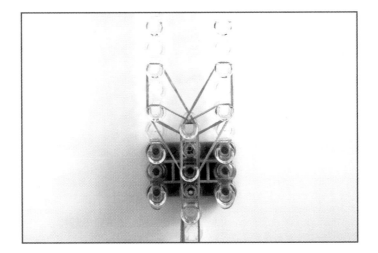

3. Like you did with the "tail," loop your bands down both outside rows,

starting from the third peg and stopping at the twenty-first peg, making sure that each band is looped across three pegs instead of two. Connect the last two pegs on both sides with a band to close the rectangle-shaped side on the loom.

4. Starting with the very end of the loom where you closed off the rectangle, work

backward and hook the bands back onto the pegs where they started. This means that each band will skip a peg, just as it did when you first placed it down.

5. Secure the loose loops on the final peg with a c-clip. Carefully remove the project from the loom. Attach the end with the c-clip to the underside of the stone to complete your bling ring!

ICE CREAM CONE

W e all scream for ice cream! This super cool project looks so good it's delicious! Hang it from a string or a key chain, or pull it out when you want your favorite frozen treat!

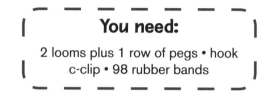

You need:

2 looms plus 1 row of pegs • hook
c-clip • 98 rubber bands

1. Set up two looms side by side plus one extra row. To lay out the cone shape, loop a band around the first middle peg, and connect it up and to the left. Loop another band to the middle peg, and connect it up to the next peg above. Loop a third band around the middle peg, and connect it up and to the right. Loop two bands across in the second row to connect the pegs where you ended the bands from the first middle peg. Loop bands around each of the three pegs you connected, and then connect them to the pegs above. Loop from left to right across the pegs where you ended your last loops. Repeat this pattern up the loom, looping bands up then across from left to right, making the cone wider every other row as shown, by adding diagonal bands when you are looping up to the next row. Continue until your cone is as wide as you want it.

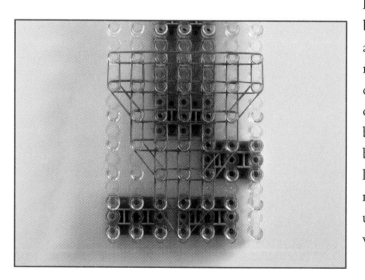

2. From your last row of cone bands, loop ice cream-colored bands around each peg in the row, and connect them to the pegs above them. Loop a row of ice cream bands from left to right across the pegs where you ended your last loops. Loop two total rows of the ice cream color, following the same looping pattern that you used for the cone. Then decrease the pattern to five pegs, and then three, as shown. Triple-loop a cap band, and put it on the top middle peg of your ice cream. As you add ice cream–colored bands, thread beads onto a few random bands before you put them on the loom.

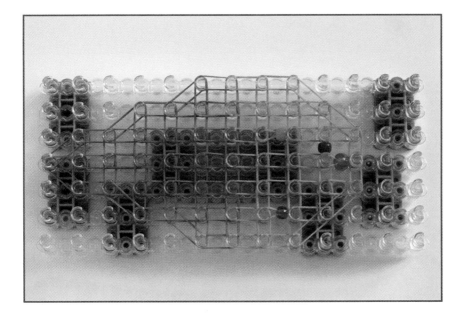

3. Begin looping your pattern, starting with the top middle triple-looped peg. Hook the band below the triple-looped cap band, and loop it back onto the peg where it began. Loop all the bands on the peg this way, then loop the rest of the row the

same way, always starting with the second band on the peg. Loop row-by-row, starting at the middle peg and working your way out before moving to the next row.

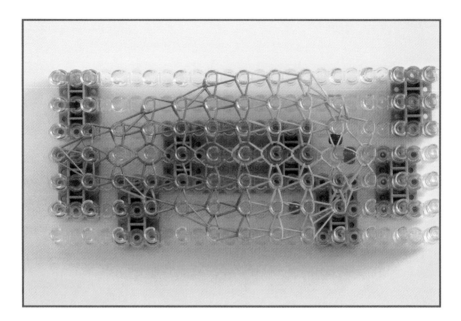

4. Secure the final loose loops with another rubber band or a c-clip. Remove your project from the loom.